NEWPORT MANSIONS

THE PRESERVATION SOCIETY OF NEWPORT COUNTY

PHOTOGRAPHY BY KURT DOLNIER

TEXT BY THOMAS GANNON AND PAUL MILLER

MISSION STATEMENT

GREAT HOUSES CONNECT PEOPLE to a nation's heritage and open windows to another age. The Preservation Society of Newport County is a non-profit organization whose mission is to protect, preserve, and present an exceptional collection of house museums and landscapes in one of the most historically intact cities in America. We hold in public trust the Newport Mansions which are an integral part of the living fabric of Newport, Rhode Island. These sites exemplify three centuries of the finest achievements in American architecture, decorative arts, and landscape design spanning the Colonial era to the Gilded Age. Through our historic properties, educational programs, and related activities we engage the public in the story of America's vibrant cultural heritage.

We seek to inspire and promote an appreciation of the value of preservation to enrich the lives of people everywhere.

Newport Mansions

ITHIN THESE PAGES you will be introduced to some of the most magnificent houses in America. You will read stories about the architects and owners of each house, and see the magnificent buildings they created, the objects they lovingly collected, and the gardens they planted – all of which make Newport a truly special place. Every one of the Preservation Society's houses has an extraordinary story to tell, and we hope that you will find the time to visit them all. They are here for your enjoyment.

Sadly, many towns and cities across America have neglected and lost much of their heritage, the architectural or landscape features that made them unique, that connected people to their past. Fortunately, Newport is different. Here in this city, preservation has been a long-standing ethic and an integral part of our identity. In fact, the story of how The Preservation Society of Newport County came to exist is an inspirational one that can serve as a lesson for citizens interested in learning how to save their own communities.

In the mid-1940s, a small group of people concerned about preserving Newport's heritage banded together to save Hunter House (1748), which was threatened with demolition. They succeeded, and with that act of civic-mindedness, the Preservation Society was born. Over the next few decades, many more preservation-minded citizens stepped forward—again and again—to protect Newport's unique assets. Today, thanks to the commitment of so many people, the Preservation Society's collection includes eleven historic sites, encompassing nearly thirty buildings and eighty acres of gardens, which together tell an incredible story of American history, architecture, and landscape spanning more than 250 years. What's most compelling is that all of it is authentic.

The Preservation Society is guided by a single mission which inspires us daily. It is a covenant not just with the past, but with the future, guaranteeing that Newport and its treasures will survive for generations to come.

Please enjoy Newport and the properties of The Preservation Society of Newport County. We hope you'll be inspired to return home and work to save your own community's heritage.

Trudy Coxe

Trudy Coxe
Chief Executive Officer and Executive Director
The Preservation Society of Newport County

The Breakers

$\mathcal{I}$F THE GILDED AGE were to be summed up by a single house, that house would have to be The Breakers. Measuring 250 feet by 150 feet, containing seventy rooms, the four-story limestone palace is as much a monument to its time as it was a summer home for Cornelius Vanderbilt II and his family.

Mr. Vanderbilt at first wanted a two-story villa to replace the original Breakers, which he bought from Pierre Lorillard in 1885 and which burned to the ground in 1892. But the first design by architect Richard Morris Hunt was scrapped for a much larger building modeled after the Renaissance palaces of Turin and Genoa. The resulting structure, covering nearly an acre of the Vanderbilts' thirteen-acre estate on Ochre Point, was more urban palace than seaside villa.

Exactly how the house came to be so large is uncertain. For Hunt, the imperial scale of The Breakers was the logical conclusion to his Beaux-Arts training and the grand manner he had developed while working on Ochre Court, Marble House, and other Newport mansions.

RIGHT | *The ornate "CV"-monogrammed north gates of The Breakers, by W. H. Jackson & Co., frame a vista to the main house.*

As the eldest son of William Henry Vanderbilt, and grandson of Commodore Cornelius Vanderbilt, who started the family fortune, Cornelius Vanderbilt II was worth more than $70 million. Nevertheless, he began work as a bank clerk and reportedly lived on his salary. He continued working long hours, even after becoming chairman of the family's railroad empire.

Work on The Breakers began in 1893 and was completed in less than two years, a remarkable feat. Hundreds of workers took part in the construction, putting the walls up stone by stone. Whole rooms were designed and built in the shops of European craftsmen, including Allard and Sons of Paris, and then shipped to Newport for reassembly.

LEFT | *A ceiling painting, mimicking the effect of a painted awning, decorates the open air upper loggia.*

ABOVE | *The majestic east facade of The Breakers faces the sea with a two-story loggia.*

LEFT | *The great hall of The Breakers, rising fifty feet, two full stories, provides a fitting entrance to the seventy-room mansion.*

RIGHT | *A vaulted alcove, off the great hall, frames a fireplace with ornamental carvings by Ellin, Kitson & Co.*

For his second home, Mr. Vanderbilt was taking no chances with fire. No wood was used in the construction. The core of the building was stone and brick with steel beams for structural support. The kitchen was isolated in a ground-floor wing and, as a further precaution, the heating plant was buried under the caretaker's cottage, several hundred feet from the main house.

For months, as the house went up, Newport society eagerly anticipated the opening of The Breakers. The interiors were finely crafted in gilded wood, marble, and bronze. Taps in the bathrooms reportedly dispensed a choice of pure rain water or healthful saltwater, both hot or cold. When the housewarming, combined with a coming-out party for twenty-year-old

ABOVE | *The ladies reception room features period
Louis XVI wall paneling (c. 1778) carved by the designer
Gilles-Paul Cauvet and salvaged from a Paris townhouse.*

RIGHT | *The most striking feature of the library
is the great stone chimney piece, originally from a
French chateau.*

Gertrude Vanderbilt, was held on August 14, 1895, The Breakers made a spectacular backdrop.

More than 300 guests were escorted into the great hall by footmen wearing the distinctive maroon livery of the Vanderbilts. The hall, rising nearly fifty feet and lined with Caen stone, provided—as it still does—a fitting introduction to the sense of space and vista that exists in all the public rooms downstairs. The east wall is almost entirely glass, affording an unbroken view across the terraces and lawn to the ocean and the distant reef that gave The Breakers its name.

Eight matching sets of doors lead from the great hall to opulent reception rooms. The two-story dining room is lined with twelve massive shafts of rose alabaster topped with gilded bronze capitals. The gray-and-gold-paneled music room has gray Ionic pilasters and furnishings and draperies of red Italian cut velvet. The cool grotto-like billiard room is faced from floor to ceiling with matched slabs of gray-green Cippolino marble.

RIGHT | *The music room, constructed in Paris by Jules Allard and shipped to Newport, was the scene of recitals and dances.*

The grand scale was continued behind the scenes in the service areas. Of the seventy rooms in the house, thirty-three were for the domestic staff. Whether in Newport or New York, Mrs. Vanderbilt reportedly could give a dinner party for 200 without calling in extra help. The kitchen, where family meals were prepared behind sealed doors so that no odors escaped into the living quarters, was a grand and efficient two-story structure. The two-level butler's pantry, where the family silverware was kept in a vault ten feet deep, held fine porcelain, china and glassware.

While the rooms inside the mansion were no larger than necessary to maintain proportion with the abundance of decoration, the house, seen from the outside, seems to overwhelm its setting. Working with such a large mass of buff Indiana limestone, Hunt did what he could to diversify the exterior, designing each of the four levels separately. Artistically, critics agreed, the east side facing the water is the most successful, primarily because of the arched double loggia that fills the space between the massive end wings. The loggias had a practical purpose as well. During the summer season they were furnished and used as outdoor living rooms.

RIGHT | *The morning room at The Breakers was used by the Vanderbilts for informal daytime gatherings.*

RIGHT | *The family dining room is decorated with nineteenth-century Louis XV-style paneling.*

BELOW | *The billiard room, a pleasing blend of grey-green marble, yellow alabaster and red mahogany, was designed by Richard Morris Hunt.*

OPPOSITE | *The Breakers dining room, richly decorated with marble and gilt bronze, is by far the grandest in Newport.*

OPPOSITE | *The grand staircase, illuminated by a John LaFarge skylight, is adorned with a seventeenth-century Flemish tapestry.*

RIGHT | *Detail of the alcove, beneath the grand staircase, decorated with a fountain and William Morris & Co. carpets.*

BELOW | *View from the hall to the stairwell, highlighting the wrought iron lanterns and balustrade. A portrait of Commodore Vanderbilt, the grandfather of the owner of The Breakers, is on the far wall.*

ABOVE | *Gertrude Vanderbilt Whitney's room features*
French furnishings selected by the decorator Ogden Codman
and portraits of Mrs. Whitney and her daughter.

OPPOSITE | *Alice Gwynne Vanderbilt's room was designed*
by Ogden Codman in neoclassical taste, and its oval contours
follow the lines of the music room below.

Despite the success of their housewarming and their great wealth, the Vanderbilts were not particularly noted for their entertaining. Mr. Vanderbilt kept busy with the family business, but still devoted hours each day to philanthropic activities. Besides his time, he donated generously to various charities, much of it anonymously. He was a devout man—he and his wife, the former Alice Claypoole Gwynne, had met while teaching Sunday school—and were active members of the Episcopal Church. The hectic schedule ceased in 1896, a year after The Breakers opened, when he suffered a stroke. He died three years later at the age of fifty-six.

Richard Morris Hunt died in Newport on July 31, 1895, before The Breakers was completed. Toward the end of his life, he expressed the hope that he would be remembered best for the picturesque stick-style cottages he built early in his career before the huge commissions became available to him. Some excellent examples of these earlier houses stand on and near Bellevue Avenue, but it is with The Breakers and his other stone palaces that Hunt's fame rests.

The Vanderbilts' youngest daughter, Countess Laszlo Széchényi (née Gladys Vanderbilt), leased The Breakers to The Preservation Society of Newport County for the token sum of one dollar a year in order to raise funds for the restoration of the Colonial-era Hunter House (1748). The popularity of The Breakers, America's greatest summer house, has been overwhelming. More than twenty million people have visited this mansion, which was finally acquired by the Society in 1972 from the heirs of Countess Széchényi.

OPPOSITE | *The kitchen, with its extensive assortment of copper pots, was the height of 1895 technology and hygiene.*

ABOVE | *The 1886 children's cottage, by Peabody and Stearns architects, hints at the picturesque informality of the original Breakers.*

FOLLOWING PAGES | *The enclosed south garden shelters formal seasonal flower beds.*

MARBLE HOUSE

*O*F ALL THE GREAT SUMMER COTTAGES
and palazzos of Newport, Marble House is
easily the most opulent. Built of 500,000 cubic feet of
cool white marble, fronted by four towering Corinthian
columns and overlooking a circular drive that sweeps up
to the front entrance, Marble House virtually defines what
a mansion should be. That is exactly what Mrs. William
K. Vanderbilt wanted when her husband commissioned
Richard Morris Hunt in 1888 to build them the finest
summer house money could buy on Bellevue Avenue.

Born Alva Erskine Smith, the daughter of a cotton
planter in Mobile, Alabama, the future Mrs. Vanderbilt
was a remarkable woman whose social skills made
her a leading hostess of Newport and New York. As a
young belle of twenty-two, Alva Smith met William K.
Vanderbilt at the resort of White Sulphur Springs, West
Virginia, and agreed to marry him. "I was the first of
my set to marry a Vanderbilt," she would say later. She
was also instrumental in raising the Vanderbilts to full
membership in New York's social elite.

OPPOSITE | *Marble House is perhaps the greatest*
nineteenth-century classical house in America.

OPPOSITE | *The floor and walls of the entrance hall are lined with yellow Siena marble and accented by a wrought iron and gilt bronze stair rail.*

ABOVE LEFT | *The marble-clad gallery connects to an oceanside terrace.*

ABOVE RIGHT | *A prized eighteenth-century French Gobelins tapestry adorns the entrance hall.*

In 1888, the Vanderbilts decided to join the summer colony at Newport. In a city where the building of a new mansion was always the object of great curiosity, work on the Vanderbilt summer house began under conditions of extraordinary secrecy. High fences prevented passersby and neighbors alike from watching the proceedings. It took nearly four years—and a reported $11 million—for Marble House to be completed. At last, on August 19, 1892, the Vanderbilts opened their house to their first guests.

Among those present was Richard Morris Hunt. The Vanderbilt commission had given him an unparalleled opportunity to practice his Beaux-Arts skills, regardless of cost. Mr. and Mrs. Vanderbilt, in turn, were so pleased with Hunt's work that they had his portrait carved in bas-relief on the marble wall of the upper hall, alongside that of Jules Hardouin Mansart, the master architect of Versailles.

The Vanderbilts had good reason to be pleased. Inspired by the Petit Trianon at Versailles, Hunt's creation was immediately recognized as a classical masterpiece, one that set the standard for similar efforts during the American Renaissance, the artistic and cultural movement inspired by a revival of Greek, Roman and Renaissance ideas and art forms. Everything in the house was done on a grand scale, from the elaborate bronzed entrance grille, weighing more than ten tons, to the ornate ballroom. Not the largest but certainly the most ornate of any in Newport, the room has carved gilt wall allegorical panels, a ceiling painting in the manner of Pietro da Cortona, and a mantelpiece of Fleur-de-Peche marble topped by bronze sculptures.

The sculptural work, and many other furnishings in the house, were crafted by Jules Allard & Sons, the fashionable Paris decorators who created the interiors for many Newport mansions. Allard, along with such Paris firms as Henry Dasson, custom-made most of the furniture for Marble House, predominantly Louis XIV and Louis XV-style pieces, in keeping with the tastes of both Hunt and the Vanderbilts.

ABOVE | *Pink Numidian marble and gilt bronze ornamentation convey a sense of opulence and grandeur in the dining room.*

RIGHT | *The gilt oak and green silk cut velvet-adorned ballroom is among the most opulent rooms of the Gilded Age.*

Marble, of course, is in evidence throughout the house. The yellow Siena marble that covers the floor and walls of the entrance hall leads to the pink Numidian marble that lines the dining room. It is difficult to imagine anyone living in this vast expanse of marble punctuated by such lush ornamentation. The ground floor rooms were generally reserved for large-scale entertainments. For day-to-day visiting, Mrs. Vanderbilt used her mezzanine level sitting room, across the landing from her husband's study.

Mr. Vanderbilt, who turned ownership of the house over to his wife upon its completion, spent only two summers at Marble House. In March of 1895, the Vanderbilts were divorced. From then on,

OPPOSITE | *A detail of the north wall of the Gothic room reveals the delicate carving of the doors.*

ABOVE | *The Gothic room was used to house Mrs. Vanderbilt's collection of rare Gothic and Renaissance objets d'art.*

William K. Vanderbilt spent most of his time on his yacht or in New York. After remarrying in 1903, he moved to Paris, where he died in 1920.

Alva Vanderbilt set out to solidify her social position by marrying off her eighteen-year-old daughter, Consuelo, to a member of the English peerage. On August 28, 1895, five months after her divorce, Mrs. Vanderbilt held a great ball to introduce a suitor, the ninth Duke of Marlborough, to Newport society.

More than 500 guests attended Alva's ball for the Duke. Footmen dressed in Louis XIV fashion led them into the main hall, which was dominated by a spectacular floral piece consisting of a large bronze fountain filled with floating lotus, water hyacinths, and fairy lamps. Fluttering about the blossoms were live hummingbirds and brightly-colored butterflies, all courtesy of Hodgson, Newport's society florist. Guests danced to three alternating orchestras in the ballroom, while French chefs prepared the dinner.

The evening produced the desired effect—at least for Mrs. Vanderbilt. The Duke proposed to the heiress in the Gothic Room, she dutifully accepted at her mother's insistence, and the two were married the following November in New York. It was the most famous wedding of the Gilded Age. Consuelo divorced her husband in 1921 to

RIGHT | *Mrs. Vanderbilt's lilac silk-adorned bedroom is decorated in an elaborate Rococo style.*

marry again, this time for love. In 1896, Alva Vanderbilt married Oliver Hazard Perry Belmont, son of the August Belmonts, and moved across Bellevue Avenue to Belcourt. Marble House was closed for twelve years, but was reopened in 1908 after the death of Mr. Belmont. Entertainment resumed, but with a different twist.

Mrs. Belmont had become a dedicated suffragist. On August 24, 1909, she opened Marble House to the public for the first time to raise money for the women's right to vote movement. Five years later she presided over an international convention of suffragettes, where she personally reassured a faltering young activist who had recently been arrested. "Brace up, my dear," she reportedly said, "Pray to God. She will help you."

Soon after, Mrs. Belmont moved to France, where she was busy restoring an old chateau near Fontainebleau when she died in 1933 at the age of eighty. She was buried

OPPOSITE | *Mr. Vanderbilt's mezzanine study groups travel memorabilia with equestrian paintings.*

ABOVE | *Mr. Vanderbilt's bedroom features a Neo-Classical bedroom suite against silk damask walls.*

in Woodlawn Cemetery in New York in a mausoleum of her own design. Mrs. Belmont had caused so many structures to be built during her lifetime, including the Chinese Tea House on her estate at Newport, that she fulfilled her youthful fantasy of rivaling the Medici as great architectural patrons.

She sold Marble House shortly before her death to Frederick H. Prince of Boston, a yachtsman, financier and president of Armour and Co. The house remained in

the Prince family until purchased from the Frederick H. Prince Trust in 1963 by The Preservation Society of Newport County. Money for the purchase came from Harold S. Vanderbilt, a renowned yachtsman who successfully defended the America's Cup three times. He was the youngest of William and Alva Vanderbilt's three children. The original furnishings were donated to the Society by the Frederick H. Prince Trust.

OPPOSITE | *Consuelo's room was designed with a French Renaissance chateau in mind.*

RIGHT | *The Chinese Tea House, overlooking the Cliff Walk at Marble House, was built in 1913 for Mrs. Oliver Hazard Perry Belmont, the former Mrs. William K. Vanderbilt.*

THE ELMS

*I*T IS NOT SURPRISING that The Elms is
distinct from the other summer palaces in Newport. When
Pennsylvania coal magnate Edward Julius Berwind chose
an architect to build his new summer house on Bellevue
Avenue, he did not, as might have been expected, turn
to Richard Morris Hunt, Stanford White, or another
prominent New York or Newport designer. Instead he
chose Horace Trumbauer, a young and relatively unknown
architect from Philadelphia.

The two men, although of different generations,
had much in common. Edward Berwind was born in
Philadelphia in 1848, the son of well-established and
prosperous German immigrants. At the age of seventeen,
he was appointed to the United States Naval Academy,
then at Newport, and began a ten-year career as a Naval
officer. After resigning his commission in 1875, he joined
his brothers in the bituminous coal business, soon taking
charge of the New York office. By the time The Elms was
commissioned, the Berwind firm was the largest supplier
of coal to the nation's merchant marine, the largest
single owner of coal properties in the United States, and
had branched out into such related fields as steamships,
railroads, and docks.

RIGHT | *The Elms, built in 1901 for*
Edward J. Berwind, is a successful adaption
of an eighteenth-century French chateau.

RIGHT | *The marble gallery and stairwell of The Elms, seen reflected in a vestibule mirror, provide a grand circulation route for the reception rooms.*

OPPOSITE | *The Louis XV-style ballroom was the focal point for summer entertaining by the Berwinds.*

Trumbauer, born in 1868 of German parentage, was a self-made man. At sixteen, he joined Philadelphia's leading architectural firm as an office boy. Eight years later, he was in business on his own. Over the next seven years, before he received The Elms commission, Trumbauer designed three large residences in the Philadelphia area, including Grey Towers, at that time one of the largest houses in the country.

Unlike most of the architects working in Newport, however, Trumbauer lacked a formal Paris education and, in fact, had never traveled abroad. Nevertheless, working from existing plans and aided by skilled French decorators, the designer in 1899 set about

recreating an eighteenth-century chateau that would inevitably be judged in comparison with the resort's other great cottages.

Mr. Berwind and his wife, the former Herminie Torrey, daughter of the U.S. consul to Italy, had been living in Newport since 1888 in a modest Victorian cottage on about one-third of an acre on Bellevue Avenue. In anticipation of building a much grander summer residence, Mr. Berwind enlarged his estate by about fourteen acres.

LEFT | *The drawing room is dominated by its ceiling painting (ca. 1740) depicting "Dawn" by the Dutch master Jacob de Witt.*

ABOVE | *The ballroom's Louis XV-style paneling is offset by a 1905 portrait of Elizabeth Drexel Lehr by Giovanni Boldini.*

In the spring of 1901, their new house nearing completion, the Berwinds went off on one of their frequent trips to Europe, leaving behind plans for a grand housewarming party upon their return. The house was ready on August 30, and the celebration began,

appropriately enough, with an eighteenth-century cotillion danced by over a hundred couples and led by Mrs. Berwind.

In the ballroom overlooking the flower-decked main terrace, Berger's Hungarian Orchestra took turns with Mullaly's Orchestra

ABOVE | *The library was designed to receive the Berwinds' Renaissance collections.*

OPPOSITE | *The airy conservatory contains important eighteenth-century statuary groups and was a setting for bridge games.*

providing a continuous flow of dance music. Outside in the garden, a brass band competed with the chatter of a throng of pet monkeys scampering about the lawn. It was an extravagant occasion for the normally reserved Berwinds and, in all, more than 200 guests enjoyed the party.

The evening was a triumph for the Berwinds. Trumbauer had provided them with a remarkable adaptation of the chateau d'Asnières near Paris, designed by Jacques Hardouin Mansart de Sagonne for the Marquis d'Argenson in 1750. Paris interior decorators

ABOVE | *The Chinese breakfast room is highlighted by its Kang Hsi-period lacquered wall panels.*

RIGHT | *A wall cistern in the dining room is adorned with a marble statue of the goddess Diana.*

OPPOSITE | *The dining room features a series of early eighteenth-century Venetian paintings.*

OPPOSITE | *Mrs. Berwind's bedroom is adorned with watered silk wall fabric and French furnishings.*

RIGHT | *The Louis XV-style gold guest room retains its original 1901 French furniture and fabric hangings.*

Jules Allard & Sons filled the house with enough period furniture, paintings, and tapestries to qualify The Elms as an instant museum. The park and formal garden surpassed most in landscape-conscious Newport. The total cost for the estate, including land, was estimated at about $1.4 million—at a time when the average wage for skilled laborers was three dollars a day.

The Elms was in keeping with the classical tastes of the time. The house is a model of classical symmetry—windows balance doors, paintings answer paintings, and mirrors are positioned opposite one another. The house is also somewhat deceptive to the eye. From the ground it appears to be two stories, rather horizontal in shape, with large sculpture groups on the parapet breaking up the roofline. Hidden behind the parapet is a third floor, containing the domestic staff's quarters— sixteen large rooms and three baths. In a similar manner, functional rooms, such as the kitchen and laundry, were kept out of sight in the basement.

Equally elaborate was the heating system used to keep the house warm and protect the paintings and furnishings during the winter. Huge coal-fired boilers provided the heat. Mr. Berwind arranged for coal to be transported to the sub-basement by means of a tunnel that surfaced on Dixon Street to the south of the estate to avoid dust and dirt. Because electricity was not available in the

neighborhood, he installed his own generator to power the house fixtures.

Grand in scale and richly-decorated as the house is, the most distinctive feature at The Elms has always been the grounds. The Berwinds lavished extra attention on outbuildings and landscaping and employed several gardeners to keep things in order.

The ten-acre park contains almost forty species of trees and a variety of shrubs and bushes, many of them manicured into trim cones and cylinders. Looking west from the main terrace, itself a formal affair with neat, ivy-lined paths and marble and bronze statue groups, the eye travels across the expanse of lawn to a row of clipped arborvitae and twin gazebos, or tea houses. Behind them lie the formal sunken gardens where beds

of begonias rest between parterre scrolls of English boxwood. Here, hidden from view of the house, are more statues and fountains.

The Berwinds, who were childless, divided their time in Newport between The Elms and their steam yacht anchored in Newport Harbor. When Mrs. Berwind died in 1922, Mr. Berwind's unmarried sister, Julia, assumed the duties of hostess. In later years, her favorite pastime was a daily game of bridge in the conservatory. It has been said that her butler was included if there weren't sufficient friends available for a foursome.

Even in summer, Mr. Berwind restricted his stays in Newport to weekends, spending most of his time at his New York office. He continued to go to work daily until he was eighty-five, three years before his death

OPPOSITE | *An overview of the garden façade of The Elms shows its commanding position over statuary-adorned terraces.*

ABOVE | *The fountain of Hercules marks the northern end of the garden's allée.*

FOLLOWING PAGES | *The Elms sunken garden was designed by Jacques Gréber and planted by the landscaping firm of Bowditch.*

in 1936. When Julia Berwind died in 1961 at the age of ninety-six, the heirs sold the furnishings at auction and the estate to a real estate developer.

The Elms was saved from certain destruction when The Preservation Society of Newport County raised enough money to buy it. Shortly afterward, the Preservation Society, through gifts and loans, managed to refurnish the house with appropriate furniture, some of it original, and The Elms was opened as a museum on August 20, 1962.

ROSECLIFF

ℛOSECLIFF IS A GLISTENING WHITE palace by the sea, a backdrop for some of Newport's most legendary parties. There is a sense of fantasy and escapism about the place, produced by its splendid architecture and the colorful people who made it their home.

Theresa Fair Oelrichs's presence—and position—in Newport were the result of a classic union between money and family name. Her father, James Graham Fair, supplied the money. As a young Irish immigrant, Fair took part in the California Gold Rush of 1849. Ten years later, following a thin vein of silver in Nevada, Fair and three partners struck the Comstock Lode, the single richest deposit of silver to be uncovered. Fair and his partners became instant millionaires, with the lode producing more than $500 million worth of silver over the next twenty years.

As one of two daughters of Fair, later a United States senator from Nevada, young Theresa Fair was able to mingle with East Coast society. On one of her trips East, in either Newport or New York, she met Hermann Oelrichs, the American agent for the North German Lloyd steamship line and a solid member of New York society. When they were married in 1890 in a spectacular San Francisco ceremony (at which the bride received a wedding gift of one million dollars from her father), the new Mrs. Oelrichs

RIGHT | *Rosecliff, one of the most refined of the Newport mansions, was modeled after the Grand Trianon at Versailles.*

64

was assured of a position in society's inner circle.

One year later, preferring the social whirl of Newport to the quieter life in San Francisco, Mrs. Oelrichs, with her sister, Virginia Fair, bought the original Rosecliff along with eleven acres of land off Bellevue Avenue, just south of August Belmont's By-the-Sea. The estate afforded an excellent view of the ocean. On the site was a mid-nineteenth-century wooden cottage built by George Bancroft, a noted statesman and prominent amateur horticulturist whose fondness for roses gave the estate its name.

In 1899, the Oelrichs commissioned the architectural firm of McKim, Mead and White to design a new summer home which,

like others of its kind, was intended primarily for grand-scale entertaining. The principal architect was Stanford White, designer of the Newport Casino and the Isaac Bell House, who responded by modeling the new Rosecliff after the Grand Trianon, the seventeenth-century garden retreat built at Versailles for Louis XIV of France.

Rosecliff, on which construction began in 1898, is a smaller version of the sprawling 100-room Trianon. Eliminating from the French design all but the main block and two flanking wings—for an H-shaped structure— White kept many of the classical exterior details, such as paired Ionic columns, arched French doors, and a multi-tiered entablature topped with statues.

The exterior walls of Rosecliff are brick, finished with near-white glazed terra-cotta tiles that resemble marble. Rosecliff conveys an impression of light and air and delicate grace. More than the other mansions of Newport, White's creation epitomizes the

lighter, more romantic side of the Gilded Age.

Once one is past the vestibule and stair hall, with its heart-shaped grand staircase, the focal point of Rosecliff is the ballroom, which occupies the entire central area of the ground floor. Measuring forty by eighty feet, it is the largest ballroom in Newport and the scene of the many lavish balls and dinners that helped Mrs. Oelrichs maintain her position, along with Mrs. Stuyvesant Fish and Mrs. O.H.P.

Belmont, as one of the three great hostesses of the summer colony. So anxious was she to begin entertaining at her new home that she moved in before work was completed, in early July of 1900. For a month she hurried the workmen along, before expelling them to take possession. As a result, the house was not completely finished until 1902, and the grounds somewhat later.

She opened Rosecliff in late August of

OPPOSITE | *The bleached oak library features a collection of coaching and equestrian oil paintings.*

ABOVE | *A Gothic style chimneypiece of colored stucco dominates the salon.*

FOLLOWING PAGES | *The Rosecliff ballroom, the largest in Newport, was the scene of many lavish balls given by Mrs. Hermann Oelrichs.*

1900 by giving a dinner for over a hundred guests prior to Mrs. Fish's Harvest Festival Ball at Crossways. Potted ferns and other florals from Hodgson, the Newport florist, camouflaged the unfinished condition of the house.

But her best-remembered party was the Bal Blanc, or White Ball, which she gave on August 19, 1904, to celebrate the Astor Cup race.

For this affair, Rosecliff was transformed into a world of white—white hydrangea and hollyhock greeted guests in the vestibule; white roses, orchids, and lilies of the valley decorated the ballroom. Women guests were instructed to dress in white only and to powder their hair. Favors were white and silver. For contrast, all

Chateau-sur-Mer

CHATEAU-SUR-MER IS A TIME CAPSULE of the Victorian age. It is a tale of two houses in one. The first, completed in 1852, was a romantic Italianate villa in keeping with other summer cottages of the time in Newport, but larger and constructed of stone rather than the customary wood. The second, engineered by Richard Morris Hunt twenty years later, was an extension and transformation of the original house into a grand chateau that hinted of marble palaces to come.

Chateau-sur-Mer was built by Seth Bradford, a local contractor, for William Shepard Wetmore, who settled in Newport after making his fortune in the China Trade. From the start, it was apparent that Wetmore wanted something more than the ordinary Newport summer home.

The house was built of rough-cut Fall River granite that gave it a sense of rugged mass not seen before in seaside villas. Three stories tall, with a four-story tower over the entrance, Chateau-sur-Mer dominated the then-open spaces of Bellevue Avenue like a large and intricate rock outcropping.

Though smaller in scale than the remodeled Chateau-sur-Mer, and almost diminutive compared to later Gilded Age houses such as Marble House and The Breakers, Bradford's house was substantial and

RIGHT | *Chateau-sur-Mer, an imposing Victorian home, was among the first of the great villas that came to line Bellevue Avenue.*

expensive enough to have been called "almost palatial" by a commentator of the time. Its construction signaled the beginning of the architectural competition among Newport's summer colonists that would keep designers and builders busy during the last decades of the nineteenth century.

Mr. Wetmore entertained on an impressive scale as well. In 1857, he gave a *fête champêtre* (country picnic) in honor of his long-time friend, financier George Peabody of London, that was attended by more than three thousand guests from Europe and America. Canopied pavilions dotted the estate, and a 175-foot canvas-topped passage led from the house to a dancing platform.

Guests danced from four to seven in the evening to the music of The Germania Musical Society, whose conductor, William Schultze, had composed a special *Fête Champêtre March* for the occasion.

The grounds, carefully landscaped with exotic trees, shrubs, and plants, were as much an attraction as the house. Although the view has since been obstructed, Chateau-sur-Mer (Castle by the Sea) at that time lived up to its name. Looking south from the 35-acre estate, guests could enjoy an ocean vista.

But the most talked about feature of the fête, reported in detail by *The New York Times*, was the sumptuous dinner served by George Downing, Newport's famous black chef. Among the menu offerings were woodcocks, plovers, snipes, fried and pickled oysters, lobster and crab, various pâtés, and galantines of turkey, ham, and tongue. Dessert included ice creams, meringues, puddings, confections molded in the shapes of Washington and Lafayette, and dark Hamburg grapes from the Wetmore grapery. It was, according to one reporter present, "probably the greatest affair of its kind ever given in this country."

The party was an auspicious start for Chateau-sur-Mer, but it wasn't long before the early history of the house was eclipsed. William Wetmore died in 1862, and the estate passed to his only surviving son, George Peabody Wetmore. By all accounts an accomplished and ambitious man, the younger Wetmore devoted his energies toward

OPPOSITE | *Low relief panel depicting Amerigo Vespucci carved by Florentine carver Luigi Frullini.*

ABOVE | *Luigi Frullini created the Renaissance-inspired walnut decoration of the library in 1876.*

building a law and political career in Rhode Island. He also undertook a major rebuilding program at the estate.

For the task, he chose Richard Morris Hunt, the Paris-trained architect noted at the time for his stick-style Victorian cottages.

Working with stone for the first time on a domestic commission, Hunt, in two building campaigns, so altered the appearance of the chateau that later observers believed the original house to have been torn down. Even as astute an observer as Mrs. John King

RIGHT | *The 1876 dining room features exuberant walnut carving by Luigi Frullini of Florence, gilt leather wall covering, and a ceiling painting by Annibale Gatti.*

Van Rensselaer may have been deceived. Writing in 1905, she called Hunt's enlarged version "one of the largest and handsomest places on Bellevue Avenue" and commented that the original house "was supplanted many years since by Le Chateau-sur-Mer," although she may have been referring to an even earlier building that once stood on the site.

The confusion was understandable. Hunt began his extensive and complicated revisions in 1871, with most of the work in the first phase completed by the following year. On the exterior, working with the same Fall River granite, Hunt switched the main entrance from its tower location on the west over to the north, where he built a grand porte-cochere, or roofed carriage entrance. In a major change to the roofline, he replaced Bradford's gently sloping gambrel roof with steeper Mansard roofs.

Inside the house, in the northwest corner, Hunt tore out the old service wing to make space for a billiard room of almost one thousand square feet. He then added a wing on the northeast side to accommodate the service area and a new high-ceilinged dining room. With the new porte-cochere, Hunt felt the need for a dramatic entrance hall. Gutting a twenty by thirty foot area on the north side, he created a three-story hall with balconies and skylight. He then added a grand staircase to complete the palatial effect.

Hunt's second building campaign several years later was a continuation of the first. At Mr. Wetmore's request for more space, he added another floor above the dining room and service wing. He also raised the Mansard roofs to towering heights.

The result was a steep-roofed monolith of stone, more overpowering and massive than even Bradford's imposing structure. Critics have disagreed about Hunt's success—and that of the house—ever since, using such descriptions as "severe" and "stern." Almost a hundred years later, architectural historian Winslow Ames referred to its "battering ram quality," hardly the words normally associated with a summer dwelling.

ABOVE | *The French-style ballroom at Chateau-sur-Mer is decorated with a mid-nineteenth-century parlor suite by Leon Marcotte.*

In one respect, the rough appearance of the house was in keeping with the masculine atmosphere inside. Under the first two Wetmores, Chateau-sur-Mer was definitely a man's world, unlike other Newport cottages where the women ruled and the men occupied themselves with business and sports.

George Peabody Wetmore died in 1921 after serving two terms as Governor of Rhode Island and three terms in the United States Senate. After the estate passed into the hands of his two daughters, Edith and Maude Wetmore, the house began to show some softer touches. Before his death, at his wife's prodding, Mr. Wetmore had commissioned his cousin, Ogden Codman, Jr., a young Boston architect, to remodel the southwest parlor in a genteel Louis XV style that moved away from Hunt's Eastlake-style rooms. The grounds were also planted with fine specimen trees, making Chateau-sur-Mer one of the finest arboretums in Newport. Olmsted Brothers, sons of the famed Frederick Law

OPPOSITE | *The northwest bedroom is known as the Butternut Room after its light-colored wood trim and furniture.*

ABOVE | *The Turkish Sitting Room reflects a mid-nineteenth-century taste for exotic Orientalist decoration.*

Olmsted, designer of New York's Central Park, were engaged in 1915 to make improvements to the entrance drive and the grounds.

Over the years, the house gradually filled with Miss Edith Wetmore's collections of contemporary paintings, drawings and French porcelain. In 1968, after the death of Edith Wetmore, the furnishings of the house were auctioned off. Many were acquired by The Preservation Society of Newport County, which also purchased the estate, preserving a remarkable house and landscape for the public.

KINGSCOTE

*K*INGSCOTE IS ONE OF THE OLDEST summer cottages left standing in Newport, a reminder of the pre-Civil War days when wealthy Southern families continued the eighteenth-century practice of spending their summers in the cool climate of the City-by-the-Sea. With its modest dimensions and gentle architecture, it is also a symbol of a less competitive time when houses were built more for comfort than for show.

The cottage, later to be called Kingscote, was completed in 1841 for George Noble Jones, a well-to-do plantation owner from Savannah, Georgia. Accustomed to country living, George Jones chose his site, two acres at the corner of Bellevue Avenue and Bowery Street, accordingly. At that time, the area was mostly undeveloped farmland, and the future Bellevue Avenue was little more than a dirt path. Situated on a high ridge overlooking Newport Harbor, the property was open to sea breezes from several directions—an important factor not only for summer comfort but for health.

It is difficult to imagine today the importance that Victorians attached to the powers of nature in preserving health. Long noted for its beauty during the nineteenth century, Newport gained a reputation for a particularly healthy climate. A *New York Times* writer went so far as to describe the atmosphere at the resort as "a kind of elixir vitae." Invalids were carried into the water at Easton's Beach daily for therapy

RIGHT | *Kingscote, designed by Richard Upjohn for George Noble Jones, is one of the earliest of the Newport summer houses.*

amidst the seaweed, and even the frequent Newport fogs were considered beneficial. Noted Unitarian clergyman William Ellery Channing, a Newporter, related how "the fogs are proverbially a good cosmetic and there is a tradition that the fair daughters of Newport owed their lustrous complexion to sleeping with their heads out the window when the mists of the sea prevailed."

Having chosen his site, Mr. Jones asked architect Richard Upjohn to design his summer cottage. Trained in England as a cabinetmaker before emigrating to America at age twenty-six, Upjohn was best known as a leading exponent of the Gothic Revival style. While his later reputation rested on his churches, including Trinity Church in New York, Upjohn's version of Gothic Revival, with its pointed gables and decorative woodwork, was well-suited to Victorian domestic tastes. After some negotiating over details—Mr. Jones wanted a larger house than the architect first proposed—work on the cottage began in 1840 and was finished the following year. The result was a charming "Rustick Gothick" house, light in scale and irregular in shape. Nestled among trees and flowers, it was picturesque without the cloying quaintness of later Victorian

"cottages." Also, contrary to popular impressions of Victorian homes as being dark and gloomy, Mr. Jones's house was light and airy, with an original cream-colored exterior, numerous large windows, and an aviary filled with large birds over the front entrance.

George Jones moved into his summer home with his second wife, his widowed mother, and two unmarried sisters. He kept a cellar well stocked with French wines and liked to entertain frequently, although on a much smaller scale than was to become fashionable later in Newport. Afternoon dinner and informal suppers were the rule, with large formal dinners the exception.

RIGHT AND OPPOSITE | *The library's furnishings reflected the King family's financial interests in the China Trade.*

Horseback riding and swimming were popular pastimes. Bathing in this era took place at Easton's Beach, a mile-long crescent of sand to the east of town. Women and their escorts were permitted to use the beach in the morning, under protection of a white flag. At noon, when a red bunting went up, women were expected to leave, presumably to be spared the sight of gentlemen in their bathing costumes, "sleeveless some and shirtless others," according to a nineteenth-century chronicler. Both sexes enjoyed picnics and chowder parties on the rocks overlooking the sea and, in the evening, charades or amateur theatricals.

Mr. Jones and his extended family continued to enjoy summers at Newport throughout the 1850s, but the atmosphere at the resort was gradually changing. In 1844, Ocean House, the first of the city's great

ABOVE AND OPPOSITE | *The twin parlors with family furnishings collected through four generations.*

hotels, went up on Bellevue Avenue across from the Jones property and began to attract steady summer visitors. Where once Mr. Jones had a single neighbor to the north, now houses were being constructed on all sides.

There were changes in the political climate as well. Newport, at one time a busy slave port, was becoming a hotbed of abolitionism, making things difficult for Southerners in general and slave owners like the Joneses in particular. When the Civil War broke out in the spring of 1861, Mr. Jones and his family left Newport and their summer home for good.

In their absence, the house was looked after by members of the King family, prominent local residents, neighbors and friends of the Joneses. In 1863, the property was sold to William Henry King, a bachelor who had made a fortune in the China Trade.

Renamed Kingscote (King's Cottage), the house would remain in the hands of the Kings and their family for more than a hundred years. When William King suffered a mental collapse in 1867, the house passed to his nephew, David King, also a former China Trade merchant. Much of Kingscote's present furnishings, including Townsend and Goddard pieces made in Newport and valuable Chinese objects, date from the first two generations of the King occupants.

The house underwent a number of changes during the tenure of David King and his wife, Ella Louisa Rives. The wooden siding was painted dark gray, the color it remains today; parquet floors were laid downstairs, and stained glass windows were installed in the entrance hall. The most important

OPPOSITE | *The Colonial Revival sideboard is offset by a family spinning wheel and Stanford White's hall screen.*

ABOVE | *The yellow Siena marble fireplace, on the west wall of the dining room, is highlighted by opalescent Tiffany glass bricks.*

change came in 1881 after the Kings decided the house, despite an earlier addition, needed more space for family and staff and for entertaining on a scale expected of prominent summer residents.

The addition was designed by McKim, Mead and White, who were at work on the Isaac Bell House (1883) and were later to design Rosecliff (1902). Instead of adding a wing to the house, which might have damaged its lines, they accomplished the enlargement by having the service wing moved about thirty feet to the northwest and inserting the addition in between. The new section consisted of a large dining room on the ground floor, which could be converted to a ballroom for entertaining, two bedrooms and a hallway on the second floor, and two nursery bedrooms and a bath on the third.

The dining room is a blend of standard and innovative materials and the most luxurious room in the house. The west wall is made almost entirely of opalescent pressed-glass bricks by Tiffany, arranged around a fireplace of Siena marble. The ceiling and upper walls, above the mahogany wainscoting, are covered with cork tiles, an innovation probably tried for its acoustical advantages as well as for its textural playfulness.

Except for a red slate roof added in 1881,

Kingscote has remained virtually unchanged to this day. David King died of peritonitis following an appendectomy in 1894, and the house was rented the next summer for use as the British summer embassy, a common practice in the days before air conditioning. The following year, Mrs. King opened Kingscote for a coming-out party for her only daughter, Maud Gwendolen King.

Maud, who married Edward Maitland Armstrong in 1901, lived at Kingscote for more than fifty years, fighting some of the same encroachment that had oppressed George Jones almost a century before. Twice she was forced to go to court to save the house, once when an adjacent shopping center was intent on expansion. Mrs. Armstrong died in 1968, leaving Kingscote to her daughter, Gwendolen Armstrong Rives. When Mrs. Rives died in 1972, she left the house, its furnishings, and a trust fund to The Preservation Society of Newport County.

THE ISAAC BELL HOUSE

*G*HE ISAAC BELL HOUSE is one of the best surviving examples of domestic Shingle Style architecture in the nation. It was built between 1881–1883 by the firm of McKim, Mead and White as a summer residence for Isaac Bell, Jr. (1846–1887), a wealthy cotton broker and brother-in-law of James Gordon Bennett, Jr., publisher of the *New York Herald*. Bennett's nearby Newport Casino was just being completed when the publisher suggested the firm of McKim, Mead and White to his sister Jeanette Bell.

BELOW | *The Isaac Bell House's façade blends picturesque massing and patterned cedar shingles.*

OPPOSITE, TOP | *Details of the dolphin bracket supports at the front door.*

OPPOSITE, BOTTOM | *The living hall combines a richly carved walnut inglenook and white oak wainscoting.*

The Isaac Bell House represents the zenith of nineteenth-century America's search for a national style. Blending English Queen Anne with New England colonial and Japanese design influences, the architects created a rallying point for a new "vernacular" style, a style that came to be known as the "Shingle Style" due primarily to the picturesque quality of exteriors sheathed in native white cedar shingles. McKim, Mead and White's early pre-mansion designs are an innovative and significant part of Newport's architectural evolution and were to have a significant impact on the later domestic work of Frank Lloyd Wright and other Modernist architects. After passing through a succession of owners, the house was purchased in 1994 by The Preservation Society of Newport County, which undertook its restoration.

CHEPSTOW

CHEPSTOW WAS BUILT in 1860–61 for Edmund Schermerhorn (d. 1891) as a summer residence and was designed by native Newport architect George Champlin Mason, Sr. (1820–1894). Chepstow is a three-story dwelling with a low, French-style Mansard roof. During its history, Chepstow has undergone several alterations but the exterior has lost little of its Victorian Italianate character.

Schermerhorn, a wealthy New York bachelor, was descended from a prominent Dutch family and was the first cousin of Mrs. William Backhouse Astor, Jr. (née Caroline Schermerhorn), a leader of Newport and New York society. Mr. Schermerhorn used the villa as a summer residence for several seasons before retiring permanently to Newport. At the time of his death in 1891, he was reported to be Newport's richest year-round resident.

The property was purchased by Mrs. Emily Morris Gallatin in 1911. She named the property "Chepstow" after a castle in Wales taken in siege by Lewis Morris in 1648 during the English Civil War. Mrs. Gallatin was a descendant of The Colonial Lords of the Manor of Morrisania, whose lands comprised more than 5,000 acres in what are now the states of New York and New Jersey, and she was also a descendant of Lewis Morris III, a signer of the Declaration of Independence.

RIGHT | *Chepstow's 1861 exterior is typical of a mid-nineteenth-century Italianate cottage in Newport.*

ABOVE | *The sitting room contains a collection of the Morris family's Hudson River School paintings.*

OPPOSITE | *The dining room is decorated with ancestral family portraits and New York furniture.*

In 1921, the Gallatins added to the property with the purchase of the adjacent George Henry Warren estate. After their deaths, Chepstow was left to Mrs. Gallatin's first cousin, Lewis Gouverneur Morris and his two daughters, Alletta Morris MacDonald and Frances Morris Perry.

Mrs. MacDonald and her family took possession of the house in 1950. Mrs. MacDonald, born Alletta Lorillard Morris, was the daughter of Lewis Gouverneur and Nathalie Bailey Morris. She was introduced to New York society in 1930 and married Byrnes MacDonald in 1935. Mr. MacDonald was president of the Sinclair Oil Company from 1946 until his death in 1959 at the age of fifty-one.

Mrs. MacDonald married Peter McBean of San Francisco in 1963. The McBeans traveled extensively, returning to Chepstow every summer. Later in life, Mrs. McBean turned her love of Newport into active support of its history by becoming a trustee of The Preservation Society of Newport County. Prior to her death, Mrs. McBean was one of the Preservation Society's foremost contributors, and she was given its most distinguished award, the Antiquarian Medal, posthumously, in June, 1986. She bequeathed Chepstow to the Preservation Society and also established the Alletta Morris McBean Foundation to "enhance the quality of life in, and perpetuate the history of, Newport."

The house contains original Morris-Gallatin furnishings together with a collection of important nineteenth-century American paintings and documents from other former Morris family residences. Chepstow is a highly evocative glimpse of the taste and collections of a descendant of one of America's founding families, placed in the context of a contemporary Newport summer home.

HUNTER HOUSE

*H*UNTER HOUSE IS A LANDMARK of Newport's commercial prosperity and artistic flowering during the Colonial Era. It is a fine example of mid-eighteenth-century Georgian architecture. Inhabited by a succession of prosperous merchants, two governors, and an ambassador, as well as the commander of the French naval forces during the Revolution, Hunter House is a microcosm of Newport's colonial and post-colonial history.

More properly called the Nichols-Wanton-Hunter House, it had its beginnings in 1748 when Jonathan Nichols bought two lots on Easton's Point from James Sheffield. As a merchant heavily engaged in sea trade, it was logical for Mr. Nichols to live on the Point. A quiet, rural area until 1711, when Quaker families began taking up residence, the Point, at the north end of the harbor, rapidly became the focal point of Newport's busy marine trade. By the mid-1700s, Newport was one of the leading ports of colonial America, with more than 500 ships involved in coastal and foreign trade, including the infamous Triangle Trade, which involved the shipping of molasses, rum, and slaves between the West Indies, Newport, and the west coast of Africa.

ABOVE | *A Colonial Revival garden with eighteenth-century plantings frames the harbor-side façade of Hunter House.*

ABOVE | *The front door pediment at Hunter House is adorned with a carved wooden pineapple, Newport's traditional symbol of hospitality.*

Like many of his neighbors along Water Street (now Washington Street), Mr. Nichols owned several ships, including at least one privateer. He also owned a number of slaves. Besides his far-flung business enterprises, Nichols was active in politics, as was his father, serving as a colonial deputy before being elected deputy governor in 1753, a post he held until his death three years later at the relatively young age of forty-four.

Upon his death, the property, including a "mansion house" along with the other buildings, was sold in 1757 to Col. Joseph Wanton, Jr., the son of a prominent Newport merchant. It was Col. Wanton who added the south portion of the house and a second chimney, giving it much the appearance it has today.

Born in 1730, Wanton, like Nichols before him, was active in both the sea trade and politics. Working for his father's firm of Joseph and William Wanton Co., the younger Wanton engaged in the popular mercantile pursuits of privateering and slave trading, as well as the growing business of dealing in spermaceti candles. Water Street at this time was a crowded row of wharves, warehouses, and ropewalks, and it is probable that Wanton continued the practice of using his house as an office as well as a home. During this period, while the activity was on the waterfront, the front of the house was considered to be the west side, facing the harbor.

As completed by Wanton, the house was a two-and-one-half story dwelling typical of its period, with a simple floor plan of four rooms per level, two on either side of a wide hallway. The walls were studded, filled with bricks for insulation, then plastered over in the English half-timbered fashion. The outer layer consists of horizontal sheaths of oak, left unpainted for years before receiving a coat of off-white paint.

The house is notable for its interior woodwork—six of the rooms have floor-to-ceiling painted pine wainscoting. The paneling in the northeast parlor is especially fine and is set off by Corinthian pilasters, painted in Wanton's time to simulate marble veined with gold. Four cherub heads over built-in cupboards flanking the fireplace were polychromed.

There is evidence Wanton installed paneling taken from other houses, which was "grained" in various shades so that the paint simulated the grains of finer hardwoods. It is likely as well that the intricately-carved mahogany staircase that rises from the hall through three stories was taken from another house, possibly the Malbone estate which burned in 1766.

Wanton furnished his house with many fine pieces from the local cabinet-making families of Townsend and Goddard, whose shops were nearby on the Point. Although all of the original furnishings are gone, the house has been refurnished with authentic Queen Anne, Chippendale, and Hepplewhite pieces made by other Rhode Island craftsmen.

Elected to the General Assembly in 1756, the year before he bought the house, Wanton rose to the position of deputy governor. For a time, with Wanton Sr. serving as governor of the colony, the family was powerful both in political and business circles. But they were loyalists at a time when sentiment was growing in favor of independence for the colonies, and as the Whigs grew in influence, the Wantons and other Tories waned.

The Wantons survived the first upheavals of the coming revolution, but in 1774 the younger Wanton lost his seat in the Assembly and a year later his father was ousted as governor. Wanton was arrested at his home on Christmas Day, 1775, released, but later exiled to his farm on Jamestown. With the arrival of British troops late in 1776, Wanton returned to Newport for the duration of the three-year occupation, eventually serving as superintendent of the colonial police for Aquidneck Island.

By now his fate was tied to that of the occupiers, and when the British withdrew from Newport in 1779, Wanton and a small band of loyalists were forced to go with them.

ABOVE | *The northeast parlor's polychrome paneling is the most important architectural feature of Hunter House.*

RIGHT | *A corner of the upstairs sitting room reveals a Newport secretary-desk and an important Newport corner chair.*

OPPOSITE | *The northwest chamber bedroom contains a significant Newport shell-carved highboy.*

By the end of the war, both father and son had died in exile. Whatever misfortunes Wanton's politics had brought him, his Tory sympathies very likely were responsible for his house being saved while others on the Point, and throughout Newport, were destroyed by marauding British and Hessian troops.

When the French allies entered Newport in the summer of 1780, they found a depressed population in a largely ruined town. Ezra Stiles, later President of Yale, counted more than 300 dwellings that had been torn down for firewood during the occupation, along with most of the orchards. Two-thirds of the residents had fled the island. Wanton's house, confiscated by the colony as soon as the British departed, was in relatively good condition and was turned over to Admiral de Ternay, commander of the French fleet, for his use. De Ternay died of a fever in the house on December 15, 1780, but the French continued to use it as a lodging and headquarters until the next year, when the fleet left Newport for Yorktown.

For years after the war, the house on Washington Street, like most of Newport, deteriorated. "Since the peace, everything is changed," a French visitor wrote in 1788. "The reign of solitude is only interrupted by groups of idle men standing, with folded arms, at the corners of the streets; houses falling to ruin—miserable shops." Wanton's house changed hands several times until, in 1805, it got a long-term owner in William Hunter, who purchased it for $5,000, a fraction of its former value.

Born in 1774, the son of a well known Scottish surgeon, Mr. Hunter was trained as a lawyer and, like his predecessors in the house, was active politically. Hunter's political career took him from the General Assembly to the United States Senate and, finally, to Brazil, where he served as chargé d'affaires for ten years between 1834–44. Although his name became associated with the house, he contributed few, if any, major changes to it during his forty-four years of ownership, other than landscaping the yard with rose and berry bushes, and quince trees.

Two years after Hunter's death in 1849, his widow sold the house to a corporation and there began another chain of owners, many of whom operated it as a boarding house. Except for numerous coats of paint inside and out and several alterations during the 1870s, in which the young architect Charles Follen McKim was involved, when the entrances were widened, the doors removed, hearth tiles added, and a back porch grafted on, Hunter House remained much as it was during Wanton's tenure. In 1945, when the house was threatened with demolition and the Metropolitan Museum of Art in New York sought to remove the paneling, Hunter House was purchased by a private group and transferred to the newly-created Preservation Society of Newport County. After several years of painstaking research and restoration, the house was opened to the public.

ABOVE | *The keeping room with its late seventeenth-century English furniture served as an informal living room and kitchen.*

Green Animals

*G*REEN ANIMALS IS ONE OF THE FINEST TOPIARY gardens in the United States. Thomas Brayton, a prominent textile mill owner from Fall River, Massachusetts, purchased the site in 1872. The white wood frame house contains vintage family furnishings and has, in part, been adapted as a small toy museum. The grounds, overlooking upper Narragansett Bay toward the north end of Aquidneck Island, contain more than eighty sculptured trees and shrubs, flower beds, and fruit and vegetable gardens. This remarkable and unique landscape was created by two generations of Portuguese-American gardeners, who fused their European horticultural traditions with American practices and climate. The most enchanting aspect, and the one that gave the garden its name, is the collection of animal figures—a camel, a giraffe, a bear, and many others—shaped from California privet. In 1973, upon the death of Alice Brayton, Mr. Brayton's daughter, the estate was bequeathed to The Preservation Society of Newport County.

OPPOSITE | *A view down the arbor path.*

ABOVE | *The Brayton house (1859) is visible
from the formal garden.*

The Preservation Society of Newport County

The Preservation Society of Newport County is a non-profit organization. Since its founding in 1945, it has come to hold in perpetuity some of America's most fascinating historic houses. The properties open to the public by the Preservation Society form an essay of America's historical and social development, from the eighteenth century through the first decade of the twentieth century. Properties such as the Nichols-Wanton-Hunter House (c. 1748), Kingscote (1841), Chateau-sur-Mer (1852), Chepstow (1861), The Isaac Bell House (1883), Marble House (1892), The Breakers (1895), The Elms (1901), Rosecliff (1902), and Green Animals Topiary Garden (c. 1860) would not survive today without the support of Preservation Society members and the hundreds of thousands of visitors who come to Newport annually to view these landmarks of America's past.

In 1945, Hunter House became the rallying point for preservation in Newport when it was learned that plans were afoot to remove its extraordinary paneling and demolish the house. Newport organized and formed a group called The Georgian Society, which purchased Hunter House. Shortly thereafter, the name of the organization was changed to The Preservation Society of Newport County.

In 1948, in order to raise money to restore the almost derelict Hunter House, the Countess Laszlo Széchényi (Gladys Moore Vanderbilt) agreed to make her family home, The Breakers, available for public tours. With revenues earned by house tours at The Breakers, the Preservation Society was able to restore Hunter House, and to look after other significant colonial structures that were threatened.

In 1962, The Elms, built for E. J. Berwind by Horace Trumbauer, was sold to a group of investors and slated for demolition. The Preservation Society was able to rally enough local support to purchase the house with donated and loaned funds. The house opened to the public shortly after.

In 1963, Harold Stirling Vanderbilt, the youngest son of Mr. and Mrs. William K. Vanderbilt, generously donated funds to the Preservation Society in order that it might purchase his family's former summer home, Marble House, from the estate of its second owner, Frederick H. Prince. Later the Prince Foundation generously contributed the original furnishings to the Preservation Society.

In 1969 The Preservation Society of Newport County's most active period of growth began. Chateau-sur-Mer, considered by many as one of the greatest Victorian houses in America, was purchased with borrowed funds. Preservation Society supporters attended the record-breaking auction of its contents and generously reclaimed many pieces of furniture integral to the highly sophisticated interiors.

Rosecliff, built in 1902 by the firm of McKim, Mead and White, was donated to the Preservation Society with its furnishings and a maintenance trust by Mr. and Mrs. J. Edgar Monroe in 1971.

The Breakers was purchased from the heirs of Countess Széchényi in 1972, more than two decades after she had opened her family's house to public tours to raise money for the restoration of Hunter House. It has become the most visited of Newport's "cottages."

Also in 1972, Kingscote, completed in 1841 by Richard Upjohn, was bequeathed to the Preservation Society by Mrs. Anthony Rives, with its furnishings and the income from a maintenance trust. Seen today, it is a unique document of one family's life in Newport through four generations, each of which left its distinguishing tastes recorded in their charming home.

Green Animals, the acclaimed Topiary Garden and Brayton family home in Portsmouth, Rhode Island, was bequeathed to the Society in 1973. The fanciful menagerie sculpted from privet, boxwood, and yew trees was begun in 1912, and is faithfully maintained today as a uniquely personal country garden.

In 1986 Mrs. Alletta Morris McBean bequeathed her family's Italianate summer cottage, Chepstow, with its family collections, to the Preservation Society. This 1861 villa provides a fascinating glimpse into the lifestyle of a prominent Newport family.

Finally, in 1994 the Society acquired the 1883 Isaac Bell House, a seminal Shingle Style cottage. The Bell House exhibits the blending of New England colonial, English Queen Anne, and Oriental design sources that characterize the fertile imagination of early work by McKim, Mead and White.

Today The Preservation Society of Newport County's properties encompass over two centuries of America's architectural, artistic, horticultural, and social history, internationally recognized for their unique position in America's heritage.